THE **A-Z** OF RUNNING ALPHA FOR STUDENTS

First published 2000

Published by HTB Publications, Holy Trinity Brompton, Brompton Road, London SW7 1JA

Printed in the UK by TPS Print, 5 Tunnel Avenue, Greenwich, London SE10 0SL
Telephone: 020 8269 1222

Contents

INTRODUCTION

Introduction

Introducing the A-Z of Alpha for Students

This manual is designed to take you through the different stages of setting up and running an Alpha course at your university or place of higher education. The following pages aim to both equip and encourage you to be able to present the Christian message in a way that is relevant to students today.

All Alpha courses are slightly different and not all of the suggestions made in this manual will apply to your course, but the aim is to provide a framework to help you get started. Try to have a good look through this manual before you start planning your course and then use it for reference as you work through the course.

Realising the need for Alpha on campus

- The church is experiencing an alarming decline in attendance within the 18-30 age group.
- Approximately 5 million people are currently in further and higher education.
- Less than 0.5 percent of them attend any Christian activity on campus.
- 2 out of 3 young people who have had contact with the established church have left by the age of 25.
- The majority of students with no church background now look elsewhere for spiritual significance.

Following a number of requests from students for help in reaching their unchurched friends at university, Alpha for Students was launched in September 1998. There is an enormous gap between school leavers and those entering the work place with many students losing their faith while at university and others sadly never coming across Christians during their years of study.

The years at university are for many students a key time to explore the deeper questions of life.

Students are surrounded by pressure: financial constraints, social pressures, complex relationships, the uncertainty of the job market and of their future. The combination of these pressures may well provoke them to ask some fundamental questions. What does the future hold? Where am I going? Does God exist? Pluralism complicates the answers to this deep spiritual hunger as the concept of 'truth' has become almost a myth. Alpha is a tool by which to present the claims of Christ in a low key but powerful manner to the millions of students who have little or no understanding of the dynamics of the Christian faith.

What is Alpha?

Alpha is a 15-session practical introduction to the Christian faith designed primarily for non-churchgoers and new Christians. The syllabus for the course is contained in the book *Questions of Life*. Most are evening courses where there is a light meal followed by a talk on a subject central to the Christian faith. Students then break into pre-arranged groups (in which they remain for the entire course) to discuss the talk in an environment where each person should feel free to ask or express whatever they wish. There is also a weekend away during which the subject of the Holy Spirit is addressed. It is a low key, non-threatening series of evenings where students from any background or belief system can ask questions about the meaning of life.

The growth of Alpha for Students in the UK

Enthusiasm for Alpha for Students has been growing since 1998 through Britain's universities with more than 100 universities and colleges of higher education running courses (see Alpha News listing of UK Student courses). Our aim is to introduce Alpha into every university and place of higher education in order that every student in the UK has the opportunity to attend an Alpha course while they are studying.

Who is running Alpha?

Alpha has been designed as a tool that any denomination or organisation could feel comfortable using. Courses are being run by a variety of student organisations, Catholic and Anglican chaplains, local churches, students, lecturers and Christian Unions. The potential of these student groups is unlimited. All over the country students are becoming Christians. Friendships are being built, communities are forming, students are supporting one another and, most importantly, students are coming into a relationship with God. The key to running a course is to do what is natural to you in your area and campus, whether it is pizza and drinks, bangers and mash or after supper donuts and coffee.

Can you run Alpha?

Christian Organisation

Various Christian organisations run Alpha courses as part of their ongoing yearly programme of events on campus and feed new Christians into their existing structures of cell groups, Bible study groups and discipleship groups.

Christian Union

The mandate of the Christian Union is to be the 'evangelistic arm of the church on campus'. This primary objective gives CUs an excellent position from which to run Alpha courses as part of their ongoing evangelistic strategy to reach the campus. Some universities have adopted Alpha for the entire CU to be part of for one term. Other CUs have encouraged hall groups to run Alpha for those interested in finding out about the Christian faith. Alternatively some exec committees have encouraged friends within the CU to join together and run the course for their friends in their rooms, flats or student houses. New Christians can be fed into the existing structures of discipleship within the CU.

Local church

Many local churches are positioned close to a university campus and may have a number of students in their congregation. Some churches have provided a venue and speakers for an Alpha course while encouraging the students to invite their friends along and lead the small groups. Local church support has proved invaluable when planning the weekend away and providing continuity for the follow-up of new Christians. Students value local church support and the partnership is vital.

Students at home or in halls

Students are the best people to reach fellow students and invite them on a course. The courses run by students in homes have been smaller but highly effective. The combination of food, video and discussion fits into a normal student evening and helps relax friends who may be nervous about coming on the course. Generally the Alpha videos are used in homes as it is less intimidating to watch a video and discuss it than have a live speaker for the average number of 10 on a course. The videos also allow the students to focus on inviting friends and praying for the evening, rather than worrying about preparing the talk.

University Chaplain

University chaplains have a challenging role. Many chaplains are not in a team and are in a campus of some 15,000 students, most of whom are not Christians. Alpha is being run by both single denomination and ecumenical chaplaincy teams in the UK. Chaplains have access to facilities and often play a vital role in supporting the CU, Christian organisations, students and churches who want to run a course. Chaplains can help with the talks while encouraging the students to lead the small group discussion groups.

University Lecturer

A number of university lecturers have run Alpha courses for their students on campus and for their fellow colleagues. Although one can combine students and lecturers in the same course, it is suggested that the small group discussions are divided between the two groups in order for discussion to flow freely.

PLANNING AN ALPHA COURSE

Planning an Alpha Course

Planning Checklist

1 Contact the Alpha for Students department

2 Attend an Alpha conference

3 Appoint an Alpha course leader and team

4 Register your Alpha course

5 Select a venue

6 Set dates

7 Order resources

Contact the Alpha for Students department

The role of the Alpha for Students department is to support each Alpha course. The department will hopefully be able to provide you with answers to your general questions about Alpha, and also help you to get up and running, by providing:

- Discounted resources – 67 percent discount on all resources for those running Alpha courses in the UK only (see page 16 for details)
- Suggested speakers – for student events and for Alpha talks during the course
- Advice on weekends/days away – offer advice on where to go, how to run it and suggest speakers and a ministry team
- Training – offer advice and the possibility of running training days for any Alpha teams

Attend an Alpha Conference

The two-day Alpha conferences are designed to train and equip you and your team to run an Alpha course. They cover the principles and the practicalities of the Alpha course and include a 'Model Alpha Evening'.

For forthcoming Alpha conferences, please see the latest edition of *Alpha News*.

Appoint an Alpha Course Leader & Team

Alpha Course Leader

The Alpha course leader should be a mature Christian. They will host each Alpha session, including the team training sessions, and will have pastoral responsibilities for the course.

Team

Leaders and helpers on an Alpha course should be people who relate easily to those outside the church; they may not necessarily have been Christians for a long time. We recommend this test: "If I had been praying for my friend to become a Christian for five years and they finally decided to do Alpha, would I want them to be in X's group?" If the answer is yes, then X is suitable to lead or help. If the answer is no, then you should look for the area where X could best serve on the course.

Registering a course

There are a number of ways to register an Alpha course:

- Contact the Alpha for Students department for a registration form
- Complete the registration form you receive with *Alpha News*
- Use the registration form on our webpage at **www.alpha.org.uk**

The Alpha Register is the list of all the Student Alpha courses running world-wide which have registered with an Alpha office.

It is updated regularly and is published in *Alpha News*.

There are a number of benefits of registering an Alpha course:

- The course listing will appear in the Alpha Register both with *Alpha News* and on the Internet. The Alpha for Students department receive a number of calls each week from people wanting to be directed to a course in their area. Using the register, people can find courses not only for themselves, but also for their friends and family
- Those running a course in the UK will receive a 67 percent discount on all Alpha resources (see page 15)
- You will receive information about special events that may be taking place

Select a venue

Based on the anticipated size of the course, select a site for the weekly meetings.

Setting

As a general rule the more flexible the setting the better. The home is the best place and is generally more palatable for the non-churchgoer. Depending on the size of your course and the rooms available it may be necessary to use an alternative. Whatever your venue we would encourage you to create a homelike atmosphere using lighting, tablecloths, background music etc.

Small group space

If you have a number of small groups, make sure that your venue has enough places for the small groups to meet in private.

Bookings

Reserve all the rooms that will be needed for every aspect of the course so that there is no clash with other events. This is especially vital if the course is being run on campus in a university room.

Set the dates

- Decide whether you will run the course over one or two terms. Turn to page 26 for ideas of how to structure your course
- Choose an evening when not much else is happening (eg not on the same night as CU, hockey training or party night on campus)
- Plan time for the two training sessions before the course starts. These are great opportunities to pray for friends, the course ahead and to bond as a team
- Training session 3 looks at the subject of ministry, and should take place during the week preceding the weekend away
- The best time for the Alpha Weekend to take place is after the talk on Guidance. However it can happen any time after the talk on Prayer but before the talk on Healing. Make sure it does not clash with any important event. From experience it is important to book the weekend early and to let everyone on the course know the dates to avoid the last minute cancellations of 'I didn't know about it!'

Order resources

67 percent discount on Alpha resources!

Students often find that money is an issue! This should not have to be an obstacle to anyone starting a course. In response to this there is a 67 percent discount on all the resources for any registered UK Alpha course for Students.

This offer is a unique discount for those running an Alpha course for Students in the UK. To take advantage of this offer you must:

- Run an Alpha course for Students ie: one for the benefit of students in further or higher education in the UK (not schools)
- Fill in an Alpha registration form making it clear you are running a course for students. We will send out your course number
- Discounted resources can only be obtained by mail order from the Alpha hotline on **0345 581 278**. When ringing say that you wish to use the Alpha for Students discount scheme for UK courses and quote your course number. You can then order all the resources you would like at this discount

NOTE: These resources are for the use of your course only and should not be sold to others.

Alpha for Students Resources

The basic resources needed to run a course for 10 guests

The A-Z of running Alpha for Students
Questions of Life
Telling Others
Alpha Administrator's Handbook
Alpha Team Training Video
Alpha Team Training Manual (x3)
The Alpha Course on Video
Alpha Manual (x10)
Searching Issues
Student Postcard Invitations
Alpha Poster Pack

HOW TO **PUBLICISE** AN ALPHA COURSE

How to publicise an Alpha Course

99 percent of people come on a course because of a personal invitation from a friend. All other methods of advertising – posters, newspapers, inserts and fliers – are simply a backdrop to the personal invitation and not a substitute. There are a variety of approaches for promoting Alpha in universities depending on the set up of the university itself. Those universities which are college or campus based can make use of the centralised nature of the halls of residence and lecture rooms. Word of mouth and personal invitations may be more appropriate for students living in a large city. Alternatively, local media or the Internet may be a more effective medium for you to use. You will know what is best for your particular university setting.

Personal Invitations

Word of mouth and personal invitations from Christian friends are generally the most effective way to publicise your course. Results of a questionnaire sent to all Alpha course leaders showed that 80 percent had found this the most effective way of encouraging students to attend their course.

Local Newspaper

How the press can and cannot help you:
- There is no guarantee you will ever get any story in the papers or on the radio because you do not pay for this form of advertising. There are certain things you can do to help, and these guidelines will show you how to do that

- There is no guarantee that your PR message or story will appear in exactly the way that you want it to. You can supply your story, but then it will be left to others (journalists and editors) to determine how it will actually appear. Student newspapers are often low on material and are more likely to publish an article if it has been written for them with a photograph enclosed

Tips on what your local media are looking for

Most local and regional press are desperate for good material. Here are a few tips to help you put something together:
- Groups of students doing something together
- Local angle
- Something that readers can relate to
- A good picture
- Speedy access to right contacts – eg people to interview
- Attributable facts and quotes
- Basic facts without complicated detail

Local/Student Radio

"The opportunities for Christians to have a voice on the airwaves has never been greater. There are nearly 250 local radio stations in Britain including many new small community stations. The audience is vast. More than 30 million tune in every week to their local commercial or BBC station. That is more listeners than BBC Radio 1,2,3,4, and 5 Live put together."

Jeff Bonser, General Sec. of the Churches Advisory Council for Local Broadcasting

As you can see, local radio could be an extremely effective way of reaching a large audience within your area. It may be an idea to put together a short advertisement. This is often quite a cost effective medium and can sometimes be used as a springboard to radio interviews or features. Contact your local/student radio station for details of their charges.

You can find out more information on radio advertising from the Radio Authority website: **www.radioauthority.org.uk** Student radio stations are often keen to hear of student activities and may be willing to interview course leaders or those who have just been on the course.

Ideas for Freshers Week

Freshers Week is a real opportunity to reach out to the student world and make them aware of the gospel. In previous years, those running courses have come up with some very creative ways of raising awareness and encouraging students to come on an Alpha course. Here are just a few examples:

Displaying posters

These are an effective way of advertising locally and will help students identify how to make contact with you. Make sure posters are personalised with the contact details of your course.

Banners

Arrange for banners to be suspended across the main street of your university campus or entrance to your university. Contact the Highways and Engineering department of your local council to obtain permission and to find out costs.

Library window displays

Often space is available for co-ordinated community projects. These spaces get booked up well in advance so enquire early.

Student Union

Approach the Student Union about placing a poster and leaving some invitations for people to take away.

Freshers Stall

Obtain permission from the Student Union to have an Alpha Freshers stall. Make use of the Alpha posters and invitations to attract attention. Hand out Alpha invitations and postcards inviting people to your Alpha course.

Fun Events

Use fun events such as putting on a play with an invitation to an Alpha course at the end or BBQ lunches, sports tournaments and dinners where un-churched friends will feel comfortable, meet other Christians and be invited to a course.

Alpha Freshers Packs

Fill small bags with a bar of chocolate, a can of coke, crisps, a party popper, a *Why Jesus?* and an Alpha invitation. Hand these out to every student. Even if they only want the chocolate, they will have an opportunity to find out more.

NOTE: Remember that any publicity on campus must have the approval of your student council. It is imperative, therefore, to approach them with your material and get the appropriate signature of approval from them before putting up any posters or banners.

Alpha Event

The Event

This could be a lunchtime or evening event to which you invite friends along. The idea is to make it informal and relaxed in order to attract non Christians to come and enjoy themselves as well as hear about the Alpha course. It acts as a teaser for your course. You could decide to have a sit down meal with jazz playing, a music event, multimedia presentation or a barbecue. Whatever you decide, make it fun and friendly.

Here is what they have done at Southampton University:
"Our Alpha Society put on two lunchtime evangelistic events on campus, consisting of a multimedia presentation (video clips from films like Trainspotting, Seven and the Full Monty, slides and music) and an invitation to the Alpha course starting the following week. We also gave out Freshers Alpha Packs containing chocolate bars, cans of coke, crisps and a copy of 'Why Jesus?'"

Gez Perry, Southampton University

A Testimony

It may also be a good idea to select one or two people to give their testimony. The best people to do this are those who have found the course of value and whose lives have been changed by God. They need to be brief, sincere, and if possible, humorous. Choose the sort of people that the majority of students will relate to.

Here are some questions that the host of the evening could ask those being interviewed:

- How did you find out about the Alpha course?
- What was the course like?
- What happened to you on the course?
- What difference has Jesus made to your life?
- What would you say to someone who has not yet done the course?

Evangelistic Event

Alpha has been used on a number of campuses as the follow-up tool to a university mission or evangelistic event, such as a carol service.

HOW TO **RUN** AN ALPHA COURSE

How to run an Alpha course

The Alpha course for students is run in exactly the same way as the traditional Alpha course. As in baking a cake, the best way to start Alpha is to follow the set recipe. With later courses there may be adaptations you need to make for a local context. Please only make changes that are consistent with the copyright statement (see page 57).

The student culture is a unique and challenging environment. It is important, therefore, to adapt the course in a way to suit you and the students on your course. The following are a number of suggestions of how to make your course more student-friendly, from creating the right environment to ideas of what food to provide.

Possible Timetables

The Alpha Course is a 15-session practical introduction to the Christian faith. As student terms are only between 8 to 12 weeks long it can be difficult to fit the course into one term.

Following are suggested course timetables which you may find useful:

In one term

Week 1	– Who is Jesus?
Week 2	– Why Did Jesus Die?
Week 3	– How Can I Be Sure of My Faith?
Week 4	– Why and How Should I read the Bible?
	– Why and How Should I Pray?
Week 5	– How Does God Guide Us?

Weekend	– Holy Spirit weekend
	– Who is the Holy Spirit and What Does the Holy Spirit Do?
	– How Can I Be Filled with the Spirit?
	– How Can I Make the Most of the Rest of My Life?
Week 6	– How Can I Resist Evil?
Week 7	– Why and How Should We Tell Others?
	– Does God Heal Today?
Week 8	– What about the Church?
Evangelistic Party	– Supper party with talk – Christianity: Boring, Untrue and Irrelevant? (either here or at the beginning of the course) to act as a teaser for the next course

Over two terms

TERM 1

Week 1	– Social: Supper party with talk (Christianity: Boring, Untrue and Irrelevant?)
Week 2	– Who is Jesus?
Week 3	– Why Did He Die?
Week 4	– How Can I Be Sure of My Faith?
Week 5	– Why and How should I Read My Bible?
Holiday	– Keep in contact with course members

TERM 2

Week 1	– Why and How Should I Pray?
Week 2	– How Does God Guide Us?
Weekend	– Holy Spirit weekend: 4 sessions (as in one term)
Week 3	– How Can I Resist Evil?

Creating the Right Environment

- Try not to use a room which is being used for another activity at the same time or which is a through-route to somewhere else
- Have something going on as they arrive. Many courses have music playing, a video playing (eg video from a recent chart show or MTV) etc
- Make it easy for latecomers to join the group without feeling awkward
- Try not to over-run the session and make it easy for people to leave on time if they wish to. Be as flexible as possible. Students can be very unreliable so be prepared for this
- Try to finish in good time and then maybe suggest going out as a group afterwards. One course said that one of their best nights was when they went out to a 70s night afterwards. This is a great way to form friendships and encourage people to come back each week

Food on Alpha

Food has always been an important part of the Alpha course. A simple but filling meal at the start of the session helps people relax, stimulates conversation and also does wonders for encouraging students to come back each week. Experience has shown that courses without a meal find that the groups do not bond as well. The meal time also enables leaders and helpers to get to know the guests in a more relaxed environment, asking questions about their daily life rather than discussing deep spiritual issues.

Often budgets can be tight, but with a bit of imagination, some easy recipes and some help from your team it's amazing what can be achieved. For ideas of what to cook you may find it a help to refer to the Alpha Cookbook for tried and tested recipes.

Or alternatively, here are a few suggestions from past Alpha courses:

- Try bangers and mash for a good wholesome meal. Easy to prepare and great to eat
- Pizza often draws students in. To make it really easy you could just order a takeaway
- If you don't have time for a proper sit down meal, home-baked cookies always go down well
- Donuts can be a good alternative and can be bought cheaply from most supermarkets
- Hot dogs are a very cheap and easy option. They take no time at all and there is little mess to clear up afterwards
- Baked potatoes with beans and cheese – cheap option
- If meals are supplied in halls, some courses offer hot chocolate with cakes and donuts

Worship on Alpha

Paul writes in Ephesians 5:19 'Speak to one another with psalms, hymns and spiritual songs. Sing and make music in your heart to the Lord'.

Depending on the setting, it is best to try and have some form of worship. We have found that although many find the singing the most difficult part of the course to begin with, it is often the part they enjoy most by the end of the course. For many, such singing is their first experience of communicating with God. It also helps people to make the step from Alpha to the church, where the worship of God is central.

Smaller courses (10 people or less) may feel conspicuous singing out loud. These courses could begin the evening with a vocalist singing two of three worship songs. This method introduces the group to worship but doesn't demand participation. Where this has been used, guests have commented on how much they enjoyed the music.

However, unless worship can be led and music played competently it is probably best not done at all. Instead you may like to listen to a couple of worship songs on CD or ask someone to come in and sing a solo for the guests to sit and listen to.

If you would like to find out more information about worship you may like to look at the Alpha Worship Pack (with cassette or CD). This is a comprehensive training resource for those wishing to introduce worship to the Alpha course. It is specifically designed for Alpha course leaders, worship leaders and music teams but also suitable for use within smaller groups for unaccompanied worship.

Prayer on Alpha

"Evangelism without prayer is like a bomb without a detonator and prayer without evangelism is like a detonator without a bomb".

Dutch Sheets, The Prayer Summit

In other words we need both prayer and evangelism to be effective.

It is invaluable to meet together as a team to pray before each session. This will not only benefit the guests but will also have the very positive effect of bonding the team together more closely.

As a group leader, you may like to pray for the people coming into your group. Pray that they will mix well and that good friendships will form. Once you have met the group, we would encourage you to pray for them daily in your own time. Opportunities for prayer with the guests come especially on the Holy Spirit weekend and after the talk on healing. Make sure that the team is prepared for this.

For more information on prayer you may like to listen to the Prayer on Alpha seminar which is available on video or audio.

Giving a Short Testimony

It is always possible to argue over facts. A personal testimony, however, makes the same point via a different route. We are all intrigued by the way other people choose to live their lives. Students will be fascinated by the insights into your life. For an even greater impact, interview one of the students themselves. An interview is less daunting for them than a monologue and enables you to shape the content of what they say.

Either 'How I came to Christ' or 'What Jesus means to me today'.
- Testimonies should be brief, honest but not shocking, specific and practical
- Make sure that God gets the glory rather than your former lifestyle
- Don't preach. Avoid church jargon
- Weave in biblical concepts and truths without reading the Bible

Content and Presentation of Talks

Film or video clips are great for raising questions, setting up an issue or illustrating a point in a dramatic, visual way.

Don't

- Explain the content of the clip. This will weaken the impact
- Use video clips just as a gimmick

Do

- Check the film well in advance. Sometime a clip isn't always as you remember it
- Make sure you (or one of the leaders) have full mastery of the technology before you use it
- Think through how you will introduce the clip and how you will follow it up immediately afterwards

Video Clips and Creative Icebreakers

1. Who is Jesus?

Forrest Gump

He runs across America 'for no particular reason'. He builds up a large following of people and then suddenly stops and makes his way home. Make the point that all of us follow something or someone (pop star, fashion, sports heroes) Do we know why we are following them?

Bethlehem Year Zero (Meridian Christmas 99)

Martyn Lewis presents the birth of Jesus in the format of a modern news programme. Makes the point well that Jesus was real and lived

2. Why did Jesus die?

The Mission

The scene where Robert De Niro has a huge weight of armour cut away by the natives he used to hunt. Make the point that this is a powerful display of forgiveness and the fact that the price had been paid.

Indiana Jones and the Last Crusade

Final dramatic scene – penitent men bow before the breath of God; walk in the steps of God; take a step of faith. Make the point that we have to take that step of faith.

Armageddon

Bruce Willis dies to save the world so that his daughter can have love. Makes the point that Jesus sacrificed his life so that we can love God.

3. How can I be sure of my faith?

Lay out several glasses of different types of drink making sure all labels are hidden. Ask the group to sample the drinks and see if they can identify the different brands. Make the point that in order to discover 'the real thing' for themselves they actually have to do something.

4. Why and how should I read my Bible?

The Simpsons

When Homer refuses to go to church and God comes down and talks to him and encourages him to do what he likes.

5. Why and How do I pray?

Video TV News

– Play this to the group and then invite short prayers relating to the areas covered

– Find any clip from a film with a child talking to a father

– Allow Christians to find things to pray for non-Christians in the group

6. How does God guide us?

Illustration

Ships and other sea vessels often use two or three fixed points on shore (eg a house, a tree and a telegraph pole) in order to ascertain or maintain their exact position. Make the point that we can often feel 'all at sea' but that God provides various ways for us to know where we stand with him.

7. The Holy Spirit weekend

Supplement the weekend by using entertaining videos outside of the talks.

8. How can I resist evil?

Return of the Jedi

Show the scene where Luke Skywalker fights Darth Vader to illustrate how to resist evil.

Chariots of Fire

It's not when you fall that you fail – get up!

The Matrix

The fight scene towards the end when Neo is fighting the agents is a good example of resisting evil.

9. Why and how should we tell others?

Light of the World

Give each member of the group a candle. Try to make the room as dark as possible and then light a candle. Use this candle to light the candle of people either side of you. They in turn light their neighbours candle and so on until the whole group have their candles lit. Make the point that the whole group can be 'lit' simply by everyone 'lighting' their neighbour.

10. Does God heal today?

The Matrix

The scene when Neo dies and is brought back to life by Trinity's loving words.

11. What about the Church?

Sister Act

Find an appropriate scene, eg the scene where the nuns set up a recreation area for the young people in the community to show the importance of church.

Mr Bean in Church

Funny example of church life.

12. How can I make the most of the rest of my life?

Dead Poets Society

Seize the day.

Back to the Future

Choose clips which show how the decisions we make affect our lives in the future.

Groundhog Day

Clips to show that each day we are responsible for the right/wrong choices or decisions that we make.

The Miseducation of Lauryn Hill

Play the last song on the album.

Saving Private Ryan

Towards the end when Tom Hanks is dying, he asks his wife to tell him he has been a good man and lived a life worthy of all those who sacrificed their lives to save him. This makes the point that we are not good and have not lived a worthy life unless it is a wholehearted run – Romans 12.

Copyright: The law is confusing over the use of specific video clips as suggested in this manual. Film and video companies have advised that technically it is illegal to show all or part of a hired film to anyone other than your family. However, in practice the law is extremely difficult to interpret. As no one has ever been taken to court over this issue, there is no established precedent. Normally distribution companies do not mind clips of their films being shown as long as:

- It is only a tiny part of the whole film
- No money is changing hands
- No profit is being made

THE ALPHA **WEEKEND**/DAY AWAY

The Alpha Weekend/Day Away

We highly recommend a weekend away. However, if only a day away is possible, that too will be effective. The teaching on the person and work of the Holy Spirit is a vital part of the course and is not to be missed.

General Information

Cost

Try to keep the cost of the weekend as low as possible. Never let money be an issue which prevents someone from attending the Alpha weekend.

Some will not be able to pay but others will be able to pay more. Ask people to contribute what they can afford – for example what they would spend in their home town over a weekend.

On Sunday morning of the weekend take a collection from all the course members, letting them know what the financial shortfall is. God always honours this principle.

Saturday Afternoon

Organise a walk or a football match for those on the weekend. Bear this in mind when selecting a venue for the weekend and make full use of any facilities available to you (eg football, cricket, netball, rounders.)

Saturday Night Entertainment

After the talk on the Saturday evening of the weekend it is good to give guests an opportunity to relax. If you have a smaller number on your weekend you may like to play a game (eg

Pictionary, Trivial Pursuit). If you have larger numbers you may prefer to have a cabaret-style entertainment evening. Ask someone to be in charge of co-ordinating the entertainments.

Speakers

If you would like someone to lead your Alpha Weekend, do contact the Alpha for Students department or your Alpha Regional Advisor. They may be able to suggest a guest speaker who you can invite. Live speakers are recommended for the weekend even if you have been using videos for the rest of the course.

Timing

The ideal time for the Alpha Weekend is between the talks on 'Guidance' and 'Resisting Evil'. It should always fall between the talks on 'Prayer' and 'Healing'. It is always preferable to have the talk 'How Can I Resist Evil?' following the weekend. If necessary switch around the talks on evil and guidance.

Venues

You may already know of a suitable venue for your Alpha Weekend. However, if you need some advice do consult:
- The Alpha for Students department or your Alpha Regional Advisor, listed in *Alpha News*
- The UK Christian Handbook (UK courses only)
- CCI Venue-finding – 01203 559099 – this is an organisation set up to find Christian retreat venues for groups. However, they cannot help for the day away

It is important to book your venue as far in advance as possible. The better venues are always booked up early.

Suggested Timetable for the Alpha Day Away

Saturday

9:15	Arrive, registration and coffee
9:45	Welcome and Worship
	Who is the Holy Spirit?
	What Does the Holy Spirit Do?
10:30	Discussion groups
11:00	Coffee
11:30	*How Can I Be Filled With the Spirit?*
13:00	Lunch
	Afternoon free
16:00	Tea – optional (or small groups)
17:00	Worship
	How Can I Make the Most of the Rest of My Life?
19:30	Finish

Suggested Timetable for the Alpha Weekend

Friday

18:30 onwards	Arrive
20:00 – 22:00	Supper
21:45	A short introduction to the weekend

Saturday

8:30	Breakfast
9:30	Worship followed by *Who is the Holy Spirit?*
10:45	Coffee
11:15	*What Does the Holy Spirit Do?*
12:00	Groups
13:00	Lunch (afternoon free)
16:15	Tea – optional!
17:00	Worship followed by *How Can I Be Filled With the Spirit?*
19:00	Supper
20:30	Revue (optional)

Sunday

9:00	Breakfast
9:45	Groups
10:30	*How Can I Make the Most of the Rest of My Life?*
13:00	Lunch

Afternoon free – but go to church together in the evening

Finally

It may be worth noting the following as a reminder of what to tell the students to bring with them. It is always a good idea to brings spares of everything just in case items are forgotten.

Don't forget to bring

- Bible, Alpha Manual and notebook
- A sketch, song etc. for revue (optional)
- Sports gear
- Waterproofs
- Towel and soap

FOLLOW-UP TO ALPHA

Follow-Up to Alpha

Expect fruit and plan

Conversion may take place in a moment, but it is part of a process. Jesus used the expression 'born again' (John 3:3) for the beginning of a spiritual life, and the New Testament speaks about becoming a child of God. While the birth of a child occurs at one moment on one day, there is a much longer process which takes place both before and afterwards.

New Christians need to be integrated into the life of the Christian community and appropriate ways of doing this will vary. You may be running Alpha in your church and so follow up is obvious. But for those running a course in their home or in halls, it is important to plan ahead to the end of your course and decide how you will encourage new Christians.

Local Church

For those not running Alpha in a church, it is very important that you are linked in with your local church. Towards the end of the course you may like to start taking your guests along to a Sunday service so that once the course has finished they are already partly integrated into church life.

In addition, a few courses have found that their local church has been really helpful particularly when hard issues have arisen in the discussion groups. They were able to turn to someone with authority for help and support.

Alpha Resources

A number of resources have been compiled with the aim of providing (new) christians with solid biblical roots for their faith and lifestyle, and to address problems and difficult issues in a clear and simple way. These include:

A Life Worth Living (available on video)

Nine talks based on the book of Philippians. Ideal for those who have just completed the Student Alpha course, and want to get going in the Christian life.

Challenging Lifestyle (available on audio)

Nineteen talks based on the Sermon on the Mount. Deals with issues such as 'How to Have an Influence on Society', and 'How to Handle Money'.

Searching Issues (available on audio)

Seven talks which tackle the seven most common objections to the Christian faith.

The Heart of Revival

Ten Bible studies based on based on the book of Isaiah, drawing out important truths for today by interpreting some of the teaching of the Old Testament prophet Isaiah. The book seeks to understand what revival might mean and how we can prepare to be part of it.

TO **CONCLUDE**

To Conclude

Alpha contains the truth of the gospel. Be encouraged as you prepare, teach and lead each session. Be prayerful and committed to the students you come across. Then they will know the truth, and the truth will set them free (John 8:32).

  We hope that this manual has shown you how Alpha can be used as an effective tool of evangelism to reach out to students around you. We have found that time and again God has honoured simple requests for him to send his Spirit amongst us. Amazing and profound changes always occur as a result. We continue to see students give their lives to Christ, be filled with the Spirit and get excited about Jesus. We hope that you will find Alpha an easy way to present the Christian message in a non-threatening manner which is relevant to students today.

APPENDICES

Appendices

Questions and Answers

What is Alpha?

Alpha is a 15-session practical introduction to the Christian faith designed primarily for non-Christians, non-churchgoers and new Christians.

What are the advantages of Alpha compared to other types of evangelism?

We are not suggesting that Alpha is the only or even the best form of evangelism. But we have found that it is proving very effective in all types of settings and cultures. For a fuller discussion of why, please see chapter 1 on principles in *Telling Others*.

Are there any special considerations when teaching the post-modern mindset?

We recognise that we live in a post-modern culture but how this translates in practice is still uncertain. We find an extraordinary mixture of mind sets in the student world, primarily between those coming from a more 'rationalist' view and those who are more 'existentialist and post-modern'. Many commentators on society have noted how the so-called post-modern generation relate to stories rather than apologetics and for that reason the New Age movement has proved so popular amongst students. Certainly we find the desire to experience God in a real way a vital aspect of Alpha, hence the importance of the Holy Spirit teaching and weekend. The material of Alpha includes many illustrations and stories which appeal to the post-modern mind, yet we also see that many of the students are more 'rational' and the logical manner with which the claims are Christ are presented appeal to them.

We would encourage you to recognise that students are all coming from different positions and a mixture of both the cerebral and experiential is vital.

Must we start with the celebration dinner?

Many people have found the celebration dinner is a great help to launch an Alpha course. However it is not the only way. You may find that it is better to use Alpha as a follow up to your University Mission.

Would you recommend doing the Alpha course with videos or with live speakers?

We recognise that the ideal is to have live speakers but we recommend that people start their course with the videos for these reasons:

- To prepare 15 talks in a term and to prepare them really well is extremely hard work
- If it is your first Alpha course there are a lot of things to organise apart from the talks
- If the course is small it is an advantage to watch the talk on video. This makes the discussion easier as the speaker is not also the group leader and the expression of contrary opinion is less threatening
- Often people move from videos to live speakers gradually

Is there a model to fit Alpha into one term?

It seems that all universities and all Alpha courses are unique. Term lengths varies from 8 to 12 weeks and so we are finding that courses are using different models to fit in with these timings (see page 26 for more details). We have found that the courses that have split over two terms have, in some cases, had a certain amount of guests dropping out over the holiday break. It is therefore very important where you place the weekend as this is often a turning point in the course for a number of the guests.

What about doing two talks in a week/night?

The whole feel of Alpha is process evangelism. It is about walking with people and what happens in between the talks is very important. So if possible try not to merge the talks unless you feel it is right for your group.

How do you encourage guests not to drop out over the holidays?

The best thing you can do is to be really organised, to plan your term and to set dates. This will help guests to know what the course involves and to fit it into their schedule.

How can we be more creative if we only have a small group?

Video clips and ice breakers can be difficult when you only have a small group. From experience, groups have found it better to listen to a thought-provoking song while everyone shuts their eyes and listens.

Do you mainly have a discussion in the small groups or do Bible study?

Our experience has been that people normally start off in their small groups by discussing the issues raised by the talk and other related and unrelated issues. When the last person in a group becomes a Christian or as the leader feels appropriate, it may then be possible to move on to Bible study. Alpha discussion groups are not Bible studies.

What do you do if one person dominates the group?

Here skill is required from the leader of the small group to draw out answers from other people and to include the whole group in the discussion (see *Telling Others*, chapter 7).

What do you do if no one in the group will say anything?

Two questions that normally get people talking in a group are:
• What did anyone think of the talk?
• What does anyone feel about the talk?
Following that, refer to the discussion questions in the Alpha Team Training manual. Do not be anxious if people are quiet for a little bit after you have asked them a question. Often it takes people time to think through what they want to say.

What happens if someone in my small group has got a really serious problem?

Each Alpha course should have a pastoral care structure in place whereby each guest is looked after by a leader or helper and each leader or helper is looked after by a pastor. As problems arise, they can go up this structure of pastoral care to the appropriate level. For those running a course at home, it is very important to link in with your local church for support. Do refer serious issues to Christian people with experience and training in that area. Don't take on something you can't handle.

Does it matter if people drop out of the course?

Obviously, it is very disappointing if people drop out of the course. However, we believe it is important to leave the guests to decide whether to come or not. If they do decide to keep coming, wonderful. If they stop coming, it is a shame, but we do not chase after them. See for example the Rich Young Ruler (Matthew 19:16-22).

Must people attend every session?

We ask those helping or leading the course to the 100 percent committed to it and to come every week and to the weekend. However, it is the opposite for those who are guests on the course: they may come and go as they wish (see Telling Others, chapter 3).

What are people saying about Alpha for Students?

"The Alpha initiative provides an exciting opportunity for every student in a British university to be made aware of the person of Christ."

Michael Ramsden, European Director of the Zacharias Trust

"I am convinced that Alpha will make a strategic impact evangelistically amongst students. I therefore unreservedly commend this conference to all who are looking to develop student ministry."

Mr Roger Ellis, Founder and Director of Fusion

"Alpha has given us an effective tool to use in reaching students for Christ."

Mr Ramsey Pigott, Director of Student Ministry, Navigators

"There have been enormous changes in higher and further education in recent years and today's student profile is most varied, demanding a variety of approaches in mission. A number of college chaplains successfully use Alpha, and learning from each others' experience at a conference such as this will be most valuable."

The Revd Paul Brice, Secretary for Higher Education/Chaplaincy, Church of England

"We have student groups in 30 universities and we are very happy to encourage sports people, who are asking questions about Christianity, to do an Alpha course."

Revd Andrew Wingfield, Digby, Director of Christians in Sport

"I think education is more than learning in lecture halls and lecture theatres. It is about the whole of life and about the human experience and how we understand that. And therefore a university Chaplain is there to ensure that the education the students are given is broader than simply a pursuit of knowledge. It is about the pursuit of wisdom; the pursuit of understanding and it is about a Christian worldview. Alpha does provide a framework of thought in which to get beyond the superficial and really engage in a very real way with students."

Rev Jonathan Brewster, Chaplain at the University of Westminster

"We started running Alpha in January 99 for the first time and we didn't have a clue what it would be like, so we were really surprised at the response that we got. We had about 22 people turn up for

our first event."

Paul Jordon, student from Koinonia Alpha for Students

"We started using Alpha in our flat. We just asked our mates around. It has been so easy, you chuck on the videos, cook a bit of food, sit down with your friends and just be yourself at home. It is the most amazing way of building community where people can relate to you. That has been the real joy for us of using Alpha. It has been pretty cool."

Al Gordon, student at Edinburgh University

"Our course was really successful because it was really based on friendships. We all got on really well and had a good time together."

Claire Alderman, student at the University of Kent

"There is a great emphasis on challenging claims and not accepting anything until you have tested it. I think the discussion group is ideal for that because after the claims of Jesus are presented then there is chance to investigate and challenge and that is an excellent model."

Andrew Latimer, student at Queens College, Cambridge

"Our experience over the last years, is that Alpha has been a more effective tool for evangelism than anything we have tried in recent years. Leaders all around the country have seen more people become Christians as a result of Alpha."

Mr Gez Perry, Navigators Student Ministry in Southampton

"We run Alpha courses and because we are very close to the university a high percentage of people attending our courses are students. This is a great area where churches can get together and

support student work on campuses and be sensitive to student issues. I think that there is a great potential for partnership. "

Rev Martin Kirkbride, St Thomas Church Lancaster

"I think that Student Alpha should be encouraged on any campus. "

Robert Otule, student at the University in London

Alpha Copyright Statement

Sandy Millar, Vicar of Holy Trinity Brompton writes:
"We have always been keen to allow individuals who are running an Alpha course the flexibility to adapt where it was felt necessary to allow for locally-felt needs and where there was the desire to retain the essential elements, nature and identity of the course. Experience has shown though that this has been misunderstood and the resulting loss of integrity in some courses has given rise to considerable confusion. Now that Alpha is running all around the world we have reluctantly had to draw up a copyright statement more tightly in order to preserve confidence and quality control. I am sure you will understand."

Alpha Copyright

1. With the exception of books published by Kingsway (in which the author is stated to hold the copyright), all Alpha resources and materials, including graphics materials, booklets and tapes are copyright to Holy Trinity Brompton.

2. In no circumstances may any part of any Alpha resource be reproduced or transmitted in any form or by any means, electronic or mechanical, including photocopying, recording, or

any information storage or retrieval system, without permission in writing from the copyright holder or that holder's agent.

3. Use of Alpha resources is permitted only when in conjunction with the running or promotion of an Alpha course. Resale, or the obtaining of payment in any other connection with any Alpha resource is not permitted.

4. Holy Trinity Brompton asks that the name 'Alpha', or names similar to it should not be used in connection with any other Christian course. This request is made in order to:
- avoid confusion caused by different courses having similar titles
- ensure the uniformity and integrity of the Alpha course
- maintain confidence in courses listed on the Alpha register

5. Holy Trinity Brompton accepts that minor adaptations to the Alpha course may occasionally be desirable. These should only concern the length of the talks or the number of sessions. In each case the essential character of the course must be retained. Alpha is a series of 15 talks, given over a period of time, including a weekend or day away, with teaching based on all the material in *Questions of Life*. If the Alpha course is adapted, the person responsible must:
- only use such a course in their own church or parish
- not allow such a course to be used elsewhere
- not publish or promote such a course

This statement supersedes all previous statements relating to copyright in any Alpha resource.

Ministry

Fear/mistrust/disbelief in super natural.

step of faith

He **will** come. Don't worry about WHAT happens- it's not you!

1) Ministry of HS
2) Biblical authoratie - library of truth.

Psalm 51 (repentance).
    -Reveal. Shine light -block? Ask
    for removal by repentance.

forgiveness, mercy, restoration.

Psalm 91 (fear) phill 4:6-7 (anxiety)
Psalm 37:5 (guidance) Rom 5:5 (love)
1 Cor 10:13 (temptation). eph 3:19

3) Dignity
   - Confidentiality.
   - <u>Affirm</u> not condemn
   Affirm person not actions.
   Don't place extra burdens on them.
4) DON'T claim anything — ARE you healed?
   No super spirituality.
   BE YOURSELF
   Harmony + unity. — denominations + churches
5) ~~an~~ Authority of church (Body of Christ
   — NOT be all + end all. Don't expect
   everything. Part of a process. play down
   expectations
6) Model for Ministry.
   - Relaxed. 2-3 (privacy) same sex
   Can't be overheard. ① Leader. ⇒
   Don't confuse.
   Give life to Christ.
   Sorry, thankyou, please.
   Spirit ∘ more. Gifts.
   Not ready — never ready
   unworthy — all unworthy

Face them + ask to come.
Silence - OK. Ask God for His advice
+ input. Don't whitter.
Text- encouraging
           Strengthening
               ing
Maybe no external signs.
Warn against temptation
He WILL come + you will see
results.
Keep in touch-go on being filled.
Get there early. 1cor 12:1-11.
What is it?
Communion? After, get everyone
involved. Take time. Disperse
People they know- Pray for GUESTS.